Terrell Davis

Additional Titles in the Sports Reports *Series*

Andre Agassi
Star Tennis Player
(0-89490-798-0)

Troy Aikman
Star Quarterback
(0-89490-927-4)

Roberto Alomar
Star Second Baseman
(0-7660-1079-1)

Charles Barkley
Star Forward
(0-89490-655-0)

Tim Duncan
Star Forward
(0-7660-1334-0)

Dale Earnhardt
Star Race Car Driver
(0-7660-1335-9)

Brett Favre
Star Quarter Back
(0-7660-1332-4)

Jeff Gordon
Star Race Car Driver
(0-7660-1083-X)

Wayne Gretzky
Star Center
(0-89490-930-4)

Ken Griffey, Jr.
Star Outfielder
(0-89490-802-2)

Scott Hamilton
Star Figure Skater
(0-7660-1236-0)

Anfernee Hardaway
Star Guard
(0-7660-1234-4)

Grant Hill
Star Forward
(0-7660-1078-3)

Michael Jordan
Star Guard
(0-89490-482-5)

Shawn Kemp
Star Forward
(0-89490-929-0)

Jason Kidd
Star Guard
(0-7660-1333-2)

Mario Lemieux
Star Center
(0-89490-932-0)

Karl Malone
Star Forward
(0-89490-931-2)

Dan Marino
Star Quarterback
(0-89490-933-9)

Mark McGwire
Star Home Run Hitter
(0-7660-1329-4)

Mark Messier
Star Center
(0-89490-801-4)

Reggie Miller
Star Guard
(0-7660-1082-1)

Chris Mullin
Star Forward
(0-89490-486-8)

Hakeem Olajuwon
Star Center
(0-89490-803-0)

Shaquille O'Neal
Star Center
(0-89490-656-9)

Gary Payton
Star Guard
(0-7660-1330-8)

Scottie Pippen
Star Forward
(0-7660-1080-5)

Jerry Rice
Star Wide Receiver
(0-89490-928-2)

Cal Ripken, Jr.
Star Shortstop
(0-89490-485-X)

David Robinson
Star Center
(0-89490-483-3)

Barry Sanders
Star Running Back
(0-89490-484-1)

Deion Sanders
Star Athlete
(0-89490-652-6)

Junior Seau
Star Linebacker
(0-89490-800-6)

Emmitt Smith
Star Running Back
(0-89490-653-4)

Frank Thomas
Star First Baseman
(0-89490-659-3)

Thurman Thomas
Star Running Back
(0-89490-445-0)

Chris Webber
Star Forward
(0-89490-799-9)

Tiger Woods
Star Golfer
(0-7660-1081-3)

Steve Young
Star Quarterback
(0-89490-654-2)

Terrell Davis

Star Running Back

Stephen Majewski

 Enslow Publishers, Inc.

40 Industrial Road   PO Box 38
Box 398   Aldershot
Berkeley Heights, NJ 07922   Hants GU12 6BP
USA   UK
http://www.enslow.com

For Libby, Luke, and Liam

Acknowledgments

Thanks to all who helped the author complete this book, especially Paul Kirk of the Denver Broncos, Claude Felton of the University of Georgia, Bob Vetrone, Sr., Jill Weakland, Jill Lipson, and Paul Steenkamer.

Library of Congress Cataloging-in-Publication Data

Majewski, Stephen.
    Terrell Davis: star running back / Stephen Majewski.
        p.   cm.
    Includes bibliographical references (p.   ) and index.
    Summary: A biography of the superstar running back for the Denver Broncos, concentrating on his sports background.
    ISBN 0-7660-1331-6
    1. Davis, Terrell, 1972– . Juvenile literature. 2. Football players—United States—Biography—Juvenile literature. 3. Denver Broncos (Football team)—Juvenile literature. [1.Davis, Terrell, 1972– . 2. Football players. 3. Afro-Americans—Biography.] I. Title

    GV939.D349 M35   2000
    796.323'092—dc21
    [B]   99-041012

Printed in the United States of America

10 9 8 7 6 5 4 3 2 1

To Our Readers:
All Internet addresses in this book were active and appropriate when we went to press. Any comments or suggestions can be sent by e-mail to Comments@enslow.com or to the address on the back cover.

Photo Credits: Courtesy Chicago Bears, p. 19; Courtesy Dallas Cowboys, p. 52; Courtesy Detroit Lions, p. 57; Courtesy of Long Beach State, p. 27; Courtesy USC Athletics, p. 13; David Silverman/New England Patriots, p. 33; Reuters/Gary Caskey/Archive Photos, pp. 40, 44, 84; Reuters/Jason Cohn/Archive Photos, p. 75; Reuters/Kevin Kozlowski/Archive Photos, p. 78; Reuters/Lou Dematteis/Archive Photos, p. 68; Reuters/Mike Blake/Archive Photos, p. 62; Reuters/Ray Stubblebine/Archive Photos, p. 9; Reuters/Sam Mircovich/Archive Photos, pp. 6, 89.

Cover Photo: Reuters/Sam Mircovich/Archive Photos

Contents

Terrell Davis runs past Green Bay cornerback Doug Evans who has fallen down on the play.

Chapter 1

Super Bowl MVP

Near the end of the first quarter of Super Bowl XXXII in January 1998, Denver Broncos running back Terrell Davis took a handoff from quarterback John Elway at the Green Bay Packers' 10-yard line. He zipped off right tackle and darted into the secondary. A crunching hit by Packers defensive lineman Santana Dotson and safety LeRoy Butler brought Davis down at the 5-yard line. He got up slowly. By the time he reached the huddle, he felt queasy and his vision was blurry. "I got hit and I was on my knees," recalled Davis. "I knew that the migraine was coming."[1]

Denver's trainers helped him off the field. Davis insisted he was fine, however, and returned to the game. Although the pain of a migraine can be crippling, Davis carried the ball two yards to the one-yard line. Tight end Shannon Sharpe noticed that Davis looked dizzy and sent him to the sideline as the first quarter clock wound down to zero.

Davis has been suffering from migraine headaches since he was seven years old, but this attack came at the worst time. The Super Bowl is the most important game of a professional football player's life. For Davis, it had even more significance because it was being played in San Diego, California, where he grew up. Now he might not be able to finish America's most-watched sporting event. "I thought, man, not at the Super Bowl," Davis said. "I prayed. I was questioning . . . why was the Man putting this thing on me?"[2]

Before the start of the second quarter, Denver's head coach, Mike Shanahan, asked his young superstar how he was feeling. "I'm seeing double and triple," answered Davis.[3] Shanahan decided to use Davis for one more play as a decoy. The plan was to fake a handoff to Davis up the middle and have Elway roll out to the right with the option of passing or running. Shanahan figured that the Packers, like most teams, would overpursue Denver's star running back. When Elway faked the handoff, Green Bay swarmed the woozy Davis and Elway waltzed into the end zone to give the Broncos a 14–7 lead.

FACT

A migraine headache affects the nerves and can be extremely painful and debilitating. Nausea, with or without vomiting, as well as sensitivity to light and sound often accompany migraines.

After his team's go-ahead touchdown, Davis had no choice but to seek treatment for his migraine. The collective hopes of Denver's fans sank as Davis sat on the bench with a towel draped over his head. Denver's trainers gave him medicine to relieve the effects of the migraine. With most of the second quarter remaining and an extended Super Bowl halftime show to rest, Davis only hoped he could return for the second half. In the meantime the Broncos, who were 13-point underdogs, had to try to stay in the game until Davis returned.

Terrrell Davis would have to overcome a migraine headache if Denver was going to win Super Bowl XXXII against the Green Bay Packers.

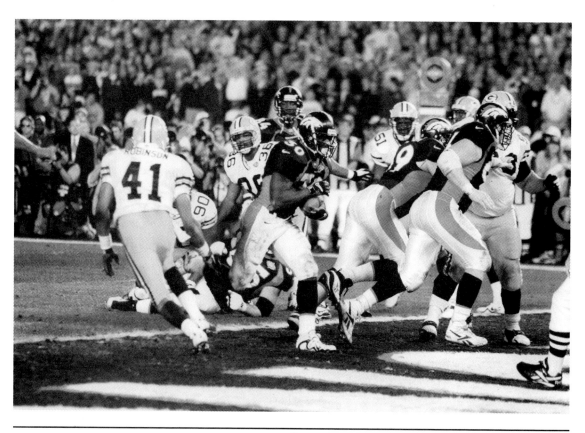

Davis's performance in the first quarter illustrated his importance to Denver's offense. After the mighty Green Bay Packers took the opening kickoff 76 yards for a 7–0 lead, it was Davis who brought the Broncos charging back on their first drive. He carried the ball six times for a total of 39 yards, including a 27-yard sprint and a one-yard touchdown run to tie the game. Davis also caught a pass for 4 yards in the drive. On Denver's next possession, the third-year running back gave the Broncos another boost of confidence with a 16-yard run. Davis finished the first quarter with 9 rushes for 64 yards.

Without Davis in the game, Denver's offense stalled. The Broncos gained just 14 yards (no rushing yards) and failed to make a first down in the second quarter. The Packers, however, were not able to take advantage of their opponent's weak offense. Packers quarterback Brett Favre fumbled in his own territory and the Broncos recovered. Although Denver could not advance the ball, Jason Elam kicked a 51-yard field goal. The two teams exchanged possessions before Favre hit tight end Mark Chmura with a 5-yard touchdown pass with twelve seconds remaining in the half. The score capped a 95-yard drive that ate up more than seven minutes on the clock and cut Denver's lead to 17–14.

In the locker room at halftime, Davis's teammates begged him to feel better and return. "I got up to him and said, 'Man, we really need you,'" recalled offensive tackle Tony Jones. "I said, 'I know your headaches are back, but you can have those headaches tomorrow. We've got a Super Bowl to win.'"[4]

Thanks to the migraine medicine, Davis was ready to play in the second half. "When I came back, my vision was back and I knew I was going to be OK," Davis said. "I knew I had to be strong for this game because if we ran the ball on these guys we had a chance."[5]

When Davis fumbled the ball at Denver's 26-yard line on the first play of the second half, it appeared that he was still sick. The Packers capitalized on Davis's mistake and drove to Denver's 9-yard line before the drive stalled. Ryan Longwell's 27-yard field goal tied the game, 17–17. This seemingly bad turn of events, however, only made Davis more determined.

After the two teams exchanged punts, the Broncos took over at their 8-yard line. Denver's coaches decided to give Green Bay a headache of its own with a steady dosage of Terrell Davis rushes. The five-foot eleven-inch, two-hundred-pound running back responded with the power of a

FACT

Super Bowl XXXII was the third most watched program in television history, with more than 133.4 million viewers in the United States. The game was broadcast to 144 countries and territories and viewed by more than 800 million households worldwide. Super Bowl XXXII was broadcast in seventeen languages—nine of those languages coming live from Qualcomm Stadium. Denver's win snapped a thirteen-game winning streak by NFC teams.

bulldozer. Whether plowing up the middle or running off tackle, Davis ground out four and five yards at a clip. He punctuated the 92-yard drive with a one-yard touchdown run to give Denver a 24–17 lead. During the 13-play drive Davis carried the ball 8 times for 29 yards.

Davis's grit and determination impressed John Elway. "In my book, he's the best running back in the league, bar none," the Denver quarterback said. "He is always breaking tackles, always going north and south."[6]

The Broncos had a chance to put the game away when Packers return man Antonio Freeman fumbled the kickoff. A touchdown for the Broncos would give the team a comfortable lead. Denver took over at the 22-yard line, but Packers safety Eugene Robinson intercepted a pass intended for wide receiver Rod Smith with eleven seconds remaining in the third quarter. The turnover breathed new life into the Packers, who drove 85 yards for a score to tie the game, 24–24. But Terrell Davis and the Denver Broncos were not dead yet.

The Super Bowl became a battle of field position as neither team could sustain a drive. With just over three minutes remaining in the game, Denver's defense forced Green Bay to punt from deep in its

By winning the Super Bowl MVP, Terrell Davis followed in the footsteps of Marcus Allen (shown here), who attended the same high school as Davis. Before Davis, the last player from an AFC team to capture the Super Bowl MVP was Allen in 1984.

own territory. A fair catch by Vaughn Hebron gave the Broncos the ball at Green Bay's 49-yard line.

Two short runs and a pass by Elway to fullback Howard Griffith brought the Broncos to Green Bay's 8-yard line. The clock wound down to the two-minute warning. Denver had a first down and goal to go, but a holding penalty on Sharpe moved the ball back to the 18-yard line. The Packers now had a good chance to hold the Broncos to a field goal. With plenty of time on the clock, however, Denver did not panic.

Elway pitched the ball to Davis, who ran to the left side of the formation. He broke free from linebacker Brian Williams and shook off defensive end Darius Holland. Davis steamrollered toward the end zone but was finally pushed out of bounds at the one-yard line by defensive back Tyrone Williams. The 17-yard run broke the will of the entire Green Bay defense. On the next play, Denver's offensive line knocked down Green Bay's defensive line like bowling pins, and Davis rolled into the end zone for his third touchdown. Denver now led, 31–24. With only one minute and forty-five seconds remaining in the game, the Packers tried to make a comeback. Behind the arm of three-time National Football League (NFL) Most Valuable Player (MVP) Brett Favre, Green Bay drove to

Denver's 31-yard line. Linebacker John Mobley, however, knocked down Favre's fourth-down pass with 28 seconds remaining, assuring the Broncos their first Super Bowl triumph.

"I'm numb. I can't even reflect. It will take a while to set in," Davis said after the win. "All I wanted to do was come here and do what I do best—run hard."[7]

Davis's effort was the one of the finest and most memorable in Super Bowl history. He had 3 rushing touchdowns, setting a new record. His 157 total yards rushing was the fifth-highest total in Super Bowl history. The fifteen-member media panel unanimously voted him the game's MVP. The last time that the American Football Conference (AFC) won in the Super Bowl, in 1984, the MVP was Marcus Allen, who graduated from the same high school as Davis in San Diego. Davis, however, took a far less glamorous path to the NFL than Lincoln Prep's most famous alumnus.

Chapter 2

Boss Hogg

In the front lobby of Lincoln Prep High School is a glass display case honoring Marcus Allen, who graduated from the San Diego school in 1978. Allen enjoyed a magnificent high-school career and won the Heisman Trophy at the University of Southern California before embarking on a sixteen-year NFL career. Lincoln athletes are now measured against Allen's amazing accomplishments. Terrell Davis joined that elite status on January 20, 1998, five days before Super Bowl XXXII, when Lincoln held a rally to retire his Davis's high school football jersey, no. 7. The atmosphere was electric. With each speaker—Mayor Susan Golding, city councilman George Stevens, Davis's former high-school coach, Vic

Player, and, finally, Terrell Davis—the cheers grew louder and louder.

It was a celebration of Terrell Davis's magnificent accomplishments in his first three years of professional football. His football career at Lincoln—unless someone exaggerates the truth— was not much more than average at best. "When I was here, I was a nerd. And not even a good nerd, at that," Terrell admitted after the ceremony.[1]

Terrell was born on October 28, 1972. He was named after Tammi Terrell, a rhythm-and-blues singer. The youngest of six boys, a typical day for him consisted of an early morning paper route through Lincoln Park, then attending school, and later going to football practice. Getting up at 4:00 A.M. for ten years to deliver papers instilled a sense of responsibility in Terrell. Lincoln Park is just a few minutes driving distance from Qualcomm Stadium (formerly known as Jack Murphy Stadium). It is in one of the poorest and toughest sections of San Diego. Terrell Davis's closely-knit family, however, helped to protect him from inner-city dangers.

As a Pop Warner (juvenile football) player, Terrell looked very much like a future Super Bowl MVP. On the football field, Terrell's Pop Warner coach, Frank White, nicknamed him "Boss Hogg," a reference to a character in one of Terrell's favorite childhood television shows, *The Dukes of Hazzard*. Other teams would shout, "Look out for number 33!" So Terrell's coach would give him a different jersey number (30, 31, 32) in the middle of a game to confuse the other team.

"Like most kids, I loved sports, all sports," Davis has said. "I played baseball, but wasn't very good at it. I was better in basketball, but not much. But football, that was another story. From the start I was another one of those wonder boys, Mr. Pop Warner."[2]

Terrell dreamed of playing professional football. He said,

> Growing up, I loved a bunch of guys—Earl Campbell, Franco Harris, O.J. Simpson, Tony Dorsett—especially Dorsett. I wore number 33 [in college] and have the same initials.[3]

Not surprisingly, Terrell's favorite professional football team was the San Diego Chargers. Posters of Chargers players covered his bedroom walls. "I wasn't a Chargers fan; I was a Chargers fanatic," he recalled. "I had all the paraphernalia in my room."[4]

Boss Hogg, however, felt like giving up football when his father, John Davis grew increasingly ill with lupus, a disease characterized by sores on the skin. A welder by trade, Terrell and his brothers fondly called him "Diddy." Sadly, he died in 1987

Terrell Davis would have to continue to dominate the league for many more years if he were to have any chance of breaking Walter Payton's all-time rushing record of 16,726 yards.

when Terrell was a freshman in high school. "I never thought my dad would go that way," Terrell said. "I was devastated."[5]

Kateree Davis, Terrell's mother, was anxious about how her children would react to their father's death. "I was worried about all my kids," she said. "I even considered counseling for them. But Terrell is strong, and he's always been a self-starter. He relies on himself."[6]

Frequent migraine headaches were another obstacle Terrell faced while growing up. They began when he was seven, and he had no idea what was wrong with him. The only way he could get relief was to find a quiet, dark place and lie down. His headaches lasted anywhere from a few hours to several days. Terrell was not diagnosed with migraine headaches until he was eighteen. Since then he has received proper medical treatment.

Terrell relied on his mother's strength to get through those difficult times. "I had some tough times in my life when things weren't going as planned," Terrell said.

> Those times were times I felt that I was alone. Well, I really wasn't alone. Every time I'd come home, my mom was there. She was my security blanket. She's the woman who would comfort me when things weren't going right.

When I was sick, she's the one who made hot tea for me and put me to bed. She's the one who looked after me.[7]

Watching his father go through a long and painful illness was difficult for Terrell. Football did not seem as important as it once was. "From what I've been told, he was an absolute legend in Pop Warner," said Lincoln Prep football coach Vic Player.

> People throughout the county knew about Boss Hogg. But the story is, he didn't play the first two years of high school because his father died at that time, and he didn't have much interest in playing football.[8]

Terrell attended Morse High School in San Diego during his freshman and sophomore years, but he did not play football. He always envisioned himself in Lincoln's kelly green and white, not Morse's blue and gold.[9] Before his junior year, Terrell transferred to Lincoln. The school transfer also offered a fresh start for Terrell, who was beginning to come out of the depression caused by his father's death.

Many great athletes have passed through the halls of Lincoln Prep. Terrell is one of twenty-eight Lincoln graduates who have gone on to play professional football (NFL, Canadian Football League, and World Football League). When Terrell decided to play football again, he was just another face in the

FACT

Lupus is a disease that affects the body's immune system. The immune system defends the body from attack by germs and viruses. More people have lupus than AIDS, cerebral palsy, multiple sclerosis, sickle-cell anemia, and cystic fibrosis combined. For most people, lupus is a mild disease. For others, however, it may cause serious and even life-threatening problems.

crowd. One of the best running backs in the NFL was not the best player on his high-school team. Besides football, he also wrestled and ran track. "I was a just another guy. I was a fourth-string running back and a second-rate talent," Terrell Davis recalled.[10]

Coach Player remembered Terrell more for his actions in the classroom than on the football field. "He was an excellent student, very mild-mannered and real respectful," Player said. "And that's unusual, especially in this culture. Our culture is extremely rowdy, and he stood out by not standing out."[11]

Talent alone, as Terrell Davis would prove in his professional career, does not make a great athlete. He transferred his do-whatever-it-takes-to-survive attitude to the football field. Davis was willing to play whatever position was necessary to help the Lincoln Hornets win. During his junior season in 1988, after transferring from Morse High, Terrell Davis played nose guard, linebacker, fullback, and kicker.

During his senior season, Terrell Davis played nose guard and fullback. He wanted to play running back or linebacker, but Lincoln had faster and stronger players at those positions. Davis proved to be a gifted blocking fullback—a skill he still utilizes as a professional. For years, Lincoln ran the I formation (an offensive football formation in which the running backs line up in a line directly behind the quarter-back), but the Hornets switched to a three-running back attack to take advantage of his blocking ability. Although Davis rarely got the ball, he made the most of it when he did. He would blast his way through would-be-blockers.

Unfortunately, Davis separated his shoulder while making a tackle on one of his kickoffs and missed almost his entire senior season. He managed to return for the final game. Even though he missed much of the season, Terrell still was a first team all-league selection as well as a second team All-California Interscholastic Federation (CIF) pick. With so many other talented players at Lincoln, however, college recruiters were not rushing to give a scholarship to a nose guard/fullback/kicker. Eight players from Terrell Davis's senior-year team were nicknamed the "90 Boys." The team went 12–2 only to lose the San Diego 2A city championship game. They received Division I-A scholarships. (The NCAA is made up of four divisions: I-A, I-AA, II, and III.) Luckily for Terrell Davis, his older brother Reggie played tailback at Long Beach State. He convinced the Long Beach coaches to take a chance on Terrell, who could play almost anywhere in a pinch.

Chapter 3

Georgia On His Mind

When Terrell Davis arrived at Long Beach State in the autumn of 1990, the legendary George Allen, who had led the Washington Redskins to the Super Bowl in the 1970s, was the head coach. As a freshman, Davis was redshirted. (College players have four years of eligibility. A redshirted player sits out one year but is still eligible to play on the varsity team for four years.) Davis was about to face the first of many setbacks during his college career. That December, the seventy-two-year-old Allen died of heart failure.

In 1991 Davis played in six games for the Long Beach State 49ers, including four starts. He was Long Beach's second leading rusher, gaining 262 yards on 55 carries. (His brother, Reggie, led the team with 636 yards.) Terrell Davis's best game came against the Arizona Wildcats. He ran the ball 11 times for 76 yards and 2 touchdowns. Unfortunately, Long Beach State lost, 45–21.

The Long Beach football program, however, could not survive the death of Allen. In the late 1980s, Long Beach rarely came close to filling its 12,500-seat stadium. Under Allen in 1990, the team finished with a 6–5 record. The excitement revived interest in the football team. The following year, under new coach Willie Brown, Long Beach slipped to 2–9. Attendance fell to an average of 3,893 for three home games. For financial reasons, Long Beach played eight road games. After the season, Long Beach State, citing budget shortages, ended its football program. If Davis had felt sorry for himself and given up, it could have been the end of his football career.

When Long Beach State pulled the plug on football, the players had two choices: stay (scholarships would be honored) or transfer without losing any eligibility with the National Collegiate Athletic Association (NCAA). Two universities, the University of California at Los Angeles and the University of Georgia, offered Davis football scholarships. After a recruiting visit to Georgia, the wide-eyed teenager decided to play for the Bulldogs.

"They took me through this big old museum-looking building with all these trophies and video screens," Davis said.

> When you touched the screens, they showed famous plays. Downstairs in the locker room, it's all red and pretty. They gave you cleats and gloves—at Long Beach we had to pay for those things. You got a game helmet and a practice helmet. They had my jersey with my name already on it. I was like, "I'm *here!*"[1]

The University of Georgia had a history of great running backs. Herschel Walker won the Heisman Trophy in the early 1980s. Rodney Hampton, who went on to become the all-time leading rusher for the New York Giants, played for the Bulldogs in the late 1980s. When Davis arrived in Athens, Georgia, their star was Garrison Hearst, who would finish third in the 1992 Heisman voting.

At Georgia, Davis learned from the team doctors that his headaches were known as migraines. Until then he had thought that everyone else also suffered from these severe headaches. "I finally had a name for it," said Davis. "Some people said to me, 'Oh yeah, I get migraines too.' That gave me a sense of security. I figured if this many people have them,

Terrell Davis (shown here) joined his older brother, Reggie, at Long Beach State in 1990.

FACT

The Heisman Trophy, awarded to the most valuable college football player of the year, is named after John W. Heisman (1869–1936). He played for Brown University from 1887 until 1889 and the University of Pennsylvania from 1890 until 1891. Heisman coached at Georgia Tech from 1904 until 1919 with an overall record of 185–68–18. He is credited with the legalization of the forward pass in 1906, the center snap, and other moves common to football today.

and they aren't dead, obviously these things aren't life-threatening."[2]

At the university, Davis majored in consumer economics. During the 1993 summer, he participated in the Housing in Action study tour in Washington, D.C. The academic program is structured around seminars with the nation's top housing authorities, finance committees, and secondary money-lending groups.

On the football field, Davis played well backing up Hearst, averaging more yards per rush (7.3 on 53 carries) than Hearst (6.8 on 228 carries). Against California State University at Fullerton, Davis had the longest run of his early career, a 61-yard burst. In that game he gained 89 yards on just 5 rushing attempts. For the season, Davis's 388 rushing yards were second only to Hearst.

In 1993 Davis became Georgia's starting running back and played well. In the second game of the season, against the eighth-ranked Tennessee Volunteers, Davis carried the ball 22 times for 131 yards, including a 42-yard run. Unfortunately, the twenty-second-ranked Bulldogs lost, 38–6. Davis's best game of the year came against Arkansas, when he racked up 177 yards on 31 carries. Davis played in all 11 games (starting in 6) and finished the season as the leading rusher for the bulldogs with 824 yards. Scouts predicted that Davis would be the third running back taken in the 1995 draft after his final college season. The decision to play at Georgia seemed to have been a good one.

"Being at Long Beach first, made me appreciate what we have at Georgia," said Davis. "Football is a well-known fact here. At Long Beach some people didn't even know we had a football team."[3]

After a successful year in 1993, Davis was determined to make the All-America team his senior season. The Birmingham *Post Herald* selected Davis for its preseason second team of the All-Southeastern Conference (SEC). A week before the start of camp, however, tragedy struck. Davis's best friend, Jemaul Pennington, was killed in a random shooting in San Diego. Davis and Pennington had been like brothers. They ran track together at Lincoln, and Pennington had lived with the Davis family during his senior year. "It was a real shock for Terrell," said Davis's brother, Reggie. "He figured it happened because he wasn't there. He felt a little guilty."[4]

Davis's problems were just beginning. During training camp, he felt a strain in his hamstring. He tried to come back before it fully healed and, once again, injured the muscle severely in the second game of the season against Tennessee. Davis missed games three, four, and five. He was not at full speed until just two games of his college career remained. "I really wanted to play in that first game," Davis said. "It never had a chance to heal. The whole year was frustrating, definitely frustrating."[5]

He rushed for only 445 yards that season. The Georgia fans were accustomed to watching the likes of Walker, Hampton, and Hearst. Thus, Davis became the focus for any criticism of the Bulldogs. Davis explained:

> When I was with Garrison [in 1992], it was fine and dandy. We were 10–2 and there was no talk about the running game. When Garrison left, all those people predicted another Garrison Hearst. I'm a totally different runner. People said, "He's not the game-breaker we need." But let me work within the system. Give me the ball 20 times a game. I can move the chains.[6]

Running-back coach David Kelly came to Davis's defense. "Fans need to get off Terrell's back," he said. "Terrell doesn't have many 60- and 70-yard runs, but that's not expected of him."[7]

To make matters worse, the relationship between Davis and head coach Ray Goff soured. "He mistook the way I practiced and the methodical way I ran for not trying, for not hustling," said Davis of Goff.[8]

When Davis became starting running back for

the Bulldogs, Goff decided to stress the passing game with his cannon-armed quarterback, Eric Zeier. Davis had more than 13 carries in only two games his senior season, and both times he cracked the 100-yard mark.

Goff has refused to elaborate on his relationship with Davis, but in 1997 he said, "Unfortunately, Terrell had some injuries at Georgia that prevented him from playing a lot. I'm happy for his success. I pull for him every Sunday."[9]

Despite the problems throughout his senior season, Davis finished the year strong. In the second to last game of the season, he was named the ESPN Player of the Game for his 25 carries and 113 yards rushing against Alabama's Auburn University, which had won 20 straight games. On the second play of the game, Davis turned a short pass from Zeier into a 47-yard gain. Behind Davis, Georgia earned a 23–23 tie. In the season finale, Davis carried the ball 25 times for 121 yards and 2 touchdowns against Georgia Tech. For the two games, his rushing yards totaled 234—more than half his season production.

The Bulldogs finished the season with a respectable 6–4–1 record. Davis finished his career at Georgia with 1,657 yards on 317 carries and 14

FACT

The National Collegiate Athletic Association (NCAA) is the group through which the nation's colleges and universities speak and act on athletics matters at the national level. It is a voluntary group of more than twelve hundred institutions, conferences, organizations, and individuals devoted to the sound administration of intercollegiate athletics. The NCAA strives to maintain intercollegiate athletics as an essential part of the educational program and the athlete as an essential part of the student body.

touchdowns. He also caught 46 passes for 529 yards and 4 touchdowns.

With his injuries and overall disappointing senior season, scouts no longer considered Davis a promising NFL prospect. Luckily, he was invited to the Blue-Gray college All-Star Game—played on Christmas Day 1994—where professional scouts flock to judge talent for the upcoming draft. Davis needed a big game to secure an invitation to the NFL's predraft scouting combine. Playing on the Gray team, he made a big play at the Blue's 10-yard line. Quarterback John Sacca pitched the ball to Davis for an apparent sweep. Davis, however, slammed on the brakes and threw the ball back across the field to Sacca for a touchdown. "We worked on it all week in practice," Davis said after the game. "Every time we tried it, it worked."[10]

During the week of practice before the All-Star Game, Davis struck up a friendship with Curtis Martin, then a junior at the University of Pittsburgh. The two players discovered that they had a lot of similarities. They were quiet, easy going, and had a good sense of humor. Of course, both shared a dream of playing in the NFL. "We just kind of bonded," said Davis. "We talked about football and life. We found that we had been through a lot of the same things."[11]

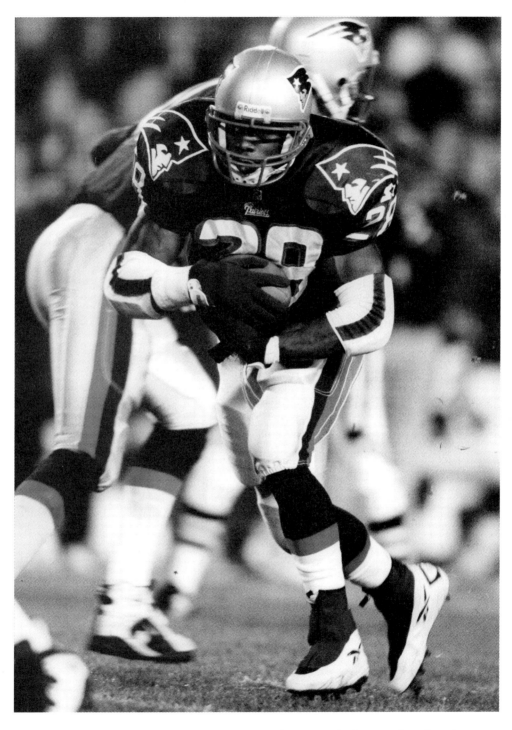

While Terrell Davis was at the University of Georgia, he became friends with Curtis Martin (shown here in his New England Patriots uniform), when he played for Pittsburgh.

Martin went on to play for the New England Patriots and the New York Jets and, like Davis, is one of the top running backs in the NFL. Back then, however, neither was considered the best running back in the country. "In our hearts, we knew we had the talent," Martin said. "We felt we could play in the NFL. But probably no one else did."[12]

Davis was invited to the 1995 NFL scouting combine, but he had a poor performance. (He ran a very slow 4.7-second 40-yard dash.) He wondered whether he would even be drafted. At five feet eleven inches and two hundred pounds, Davis had decent but not extraordinary size. Knowing his stock had fallen for the 1995 NFL draft, Davis caught up on some sleep in his Georgia apartment rather than watch the draft on television. The Denver Broncos selected him in the sixth round. There were 195 players, including 20 running backs, picked before Davis. He was silently outraged and dedicated himself to proving the scouts wrong.

"You've never seen a kid prepare harder for what was ahead of him, both physically and mentally," said Georgia's running-back coach David Kelly. "He almost worked himself sick. It became a crusade."[13]

It is unusual for sixth-round draft choices to survive NFL training camps. Davis knew he faced an uphill battle. "I was thinking, 'When you get drafted this late, all you are is camp meat,'" said Davis.[14]

Camp meat is what NFL players call the low-round draft choices who have little or no chance of making the team. But it soon became clear at Denver's training camp that Davis was anything but camp meat.

Chapter 4

Rookie

When the Denver Broncos selected Terrell Davis in the 1995 draft, Mike Shanahan was beginning his first year as head coach in Denver. He planned to install a "West Coast" style offense, which emphasized the short passing game. To be successful, this offense requires versatile running backs who can catch as well as block. Shanahan would soon find that Davis was a powerful runner, a sure-handed receiver, and a skilled blocker. For now, however, Davis would be lucky to make the team as a third-down substitute and a special-teams player.

It did not take long for Terrell Davis to make his presence known to the Broncos. In Denver's first preseason game against the defending Super Bowl champion San Francisco 49ers, Davis flew down the field on special teams and exploded into San Francisco's return man, Tyronne Drakeford. On offense, Davis was Denver's leading rusher, carrying the ball 11 times for 46 yards and one touchdown. The Broncos won that game, 24–10.

As the preseason progressed, Davis went from being a longshot for making the team to competing for the starting running back position. "He's got a chance to help us this season," Coach Shanahan said. "He's competing for a starting job right now. That doesn't happen very often with a sixth-round pick. But he's picked up the system quickly."[1]

In the final exhibition game against the Dallas Cowboys, Davis rushed for 73 yards on 10 carries as Denver won, 20–17. All his hard work since the draft had paid off. Davis became Denver's first rookie to start the season at tailback since 1989. "The big thing with him is yardage after the first hit," said Ted Sundquist, director of college scouting for the Broncos. "He does keep his legs moving and he has a good body—lean. He has fullback strength in a tailback's body."[2] (A fullback is typically big and strong. A tailback is typically smaller and quicker. A tailback with fullback strength is an imposing player.)

As the starting running back for the Broncos,

Davis became an instant celebrity in the Denver area. Television and radio stations offered him weekly guest spots. The ever-level-headed Davis, however, refused to be seduced by the bright lights of stardom. "I thought it would be a big distraction," he recalled. "I didn't need to ease up."[3]

Davis certainly did not let up during Denver's first regular-season game against the Buffalo Bills. He carried the ball 20 times for 70 yards. He also scored one touchdown to help Denver to a 22–7 victory. After Davis scored his first professional touchdown, he simply dropped the ball in the end zone and jogged to the bench rather than showboat with an emphatic spike, displaying the poise of a seasoned veteran. Against the Washington Redskins in game three, Davis tied a Denver record with 3 touchdowns (2 rushing, one receiving). Denver's 38–31 win against the Redskins improved the team's record to 2–1.

Although Davis's overall statistics against the Redskins were not spectacular, he considers it one of his best performances. "It was the most complete game I've ever had," he said. "I caught the ball seven times for . . . yards, ran the ball [13 times] for . . . yards, had to run-block, had to pass-block. I left the game feeling good, even though I didn't break 100 yards."[4]

FACT

Football is not just played on offense and defense. Kicking and punting are two other important parts of the game. Players who are on the field during kickoffs, punts, field goal attempts, and extra point attempts are referred to as special teams players.

The most anticipated game so far in Davis's young professional career came in late September 1995 against the Chargers in his hometown of San Diego. He grew up a fanatical Chargers supporter. Now he returned with the goal of defeating the team he once adored. Unfortunately for Davis, he carried the ball just 7 times for 27 yards and the Broncos lost. "It was not quite what I envisioned," he said following the game. "It was nice to come home and see my family, but this was a business trip and we came out here to win a game, and we didn't do that."[5]

Another emotionally important game for Terrell Davis came against the New England Patriots. New England's starting running back was Curtis Martin. He and Davis had become good friends when they had met at the 1994 Blue-Gray Game. For Davis and the Broncos, the outcome was much better than the San Diego game had been, as Denver won in a romp, 37–3. Davis helped the Broncos on their first scoring drive with a 32-yard run. Later, during the first quarter, he scored on a one-yard touchdown plunge.

Another milestone in Davis's rookie year came when he faced the Kansas City Chiefs. Marcus Allen, who had attended the same high school as Davis, was Kansas City's running back. The crafty

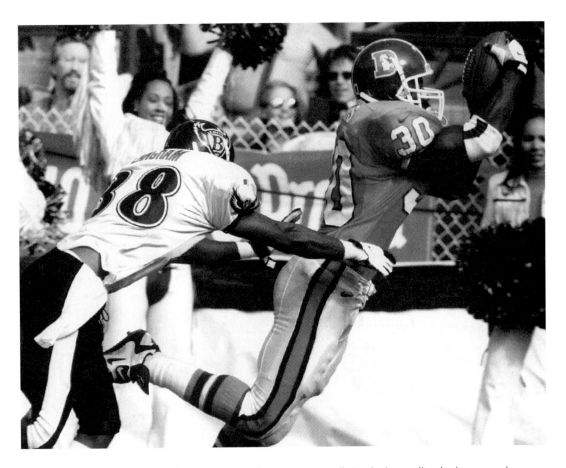

Although he was a low-round draft choice, Terrell Davis immediately impressed Denver's first-year coach, Mike Shanahan. Davis played so well in the preseason that Shanahan named him the starting tailback.

veteran, however, did not let the emerging young star upstage him. Allen tallied just his second regular-season 100-yard rushing day since 1988. He also scored his one hundredth career rushing touchdown to help the Chiefs win, 21–7.

After the game, Davis tried to meet Allen, who was one of his childhood idols. "I wanted to meet him finally," he said. "But he was gone [into Kansas City's locker room] before I could stop him."[6]

The goal of every NFL team is to have its starting running back rush for 100 yards (or more) in a game. A rushing total of 100 yards means that a team is running the ball well. Many coaches believe that a good running game is essential to winning. Running allows a team to control the clock. (The other team cannot score without the ball.) Rushing is also safer than passing (less chance of turning the ball over). Davis had yet to reach the 100-yard plateau in his short professional career. It seemed unlikely that he would do so in Denver's ninth game of the season against the Arizona Cardinals. The Cardinals were coached by Buddy Ryan who prided himself on stopping the run.

The Cardinals, however, were struggling, and the Broncos immediately went to the ground. Davis ran for 60 of Denver's 69-yard opening drive, which he capped with a 5-yard touchdown run. Denver

FACT

Once a year, usually in April, the NFL conducts a draft of college players. The team with the worst record from the previous season picks first and the Super Bowl winner selects last. This scenario is repeated seven times in what are called rounds. A player selected in the first round is referred to as a first-round draft pick. When a player is selected by a team, he must sign a contract with that franchise or sit out the season, unless he is traded.

never looked back and went on to an impressive 38–6 rout. The win improved Denver's record to 5–4. Davis finished the game with 135 yards on 22 carries. It was the most yards on the ground at Mile High Stadium (Denver's home field) by a Bronco player since Otis Armstrong had rushed for 183 yards in 1974.

Two weeks later, against the San Diego Chargers, Davis played in a game that was a turning point not only in his career but also in the identity of the Denver franchise. Since John Elway began playing quarterback for Denver in 1983, the fortunes of the Broncos rode on his broad shoulders. If Elway had a good game, Denver had a chance to win. With his athletic scrambling ability and cannon arm, Elway often won games seemingly by magic. So when Denver took possession at its 33-yard line with the score tied 27–27, it seemed likely that the Broncos would go to the passing game. With only three minutes and forty-three seconds to play, the south end zone scoreboard flashed the following message: "John Elway—28 game-winning drives in 4th quarter, most in NFL history."

On the first play, Elway handed off to Davis, who gained 19 yards off left tackle. Davis followed that with runs of 9 and 10 yards up the middle. The two-minute warning stopped play with Denver at San Diego's 29-yard line. Again, Davis ran, this time for 4 yards, then for 2. Even on third-and-four from the 23-yard line, Elway did not throw. He handed the ball to Davis, who crashed through the line for 9 more yards. Broncos kicker Jason Elam trotted out onto the field and secured a 30–27 victory for the Broncos with an easy 32-yard field goal.

Elway had not passed once. Davis ran six straight times for 53 yards. He showed no mercy for the team he once worshiped. "I had all their posters, and I cried every time they lost," Davis said. "I put that all behind me once I got on the field. I wanted the ball on the final drive."[7]

In all, Davis carried the ball 30 times for 176 yards and one touchdown. No one else rushed the football for the Broncos that day. It was the third best rushing performance in Broncos history. More important, it ushered in a new era. Denver no longer had to rely solely on the arm of John Elway to win. The running power of Davis added another dimension to the team. "The successful teams can run the football," said Coach Shanahan. "If the only weapon we had was John [Elway] throwing the ball to our wide receivers downfield, when you have an off day or bad weather, all of the sudden you're in there for a big loss."[8]

Terrell Davis gave the Broncos another dimension that they sorely lacked. Without Davis, they had to rely solely on the arm of quarterback John Elway.

Only one question remained after the game: Was this Elway's twenty-ninth game-winning drive or Davis's first? "Doesn't matter," Davis answered. "I'm living in a dream right now. When the coaches have that much confidence in you, you just have to prove them right."[9]

With 883 yards on the ground, Davis was the AFC's number-two rusher behind Seattle's Chris Warren (977). In the blink of an eye, Davis had gone from being an obscure draft pick to becoming a candidate for Rookie of the Year honors. "He's the best rookie back I've ever been around," said Shanahan. "He's wise beyond his years."[10]

While Davis was enjoying an outstanding rookie season, Denver was stuck in a win-one, lose-one cycle. With a 6–5 record, however, the Broncos had a chance to make the playoffs if they could win their remaining games. Davis did all he could to help Denver beat the Houston Oilers. He ran the ball 19 times for 110 yards, including a 60-yard touchdown run. Denver, however, lost the game.

The following week Denver beat the Jacksonville Jaguars, 31–23, improving its record to 7–6 and keeping its playoff hopes alive. Davis ran 21 times for 84 yards. It looked as if the Broncos would win two in a row when they jumped out to a 20–0 lead against the Seattle Seahawks. But then disaster struck. After gaining 40 yards on just five carries, Davis suffered a torn right hamstring in the first quarter and had to leave the game. Seattle rallied and won the game, 31–27.

The injury forced Davis to miss the final two games of the season. At the time, he led the AFC in total yards from scrimmage (rushing and receiving yards combined). Without Davis, Denver finished with an 8–8 record and did not make the playoffs. It was a frustrating end to the season, but with Davis at running back the future looked bright for the Denver Broncos.

Davis finished his rookie season with 1,117 yards rushing, the third-best total in the AFC and the ninth-best total in the NFL. He was the lowest-drafted player to rush for 1,000 yards as a rookie in NFL history. Davis's running style of following his blocks, hitting the hole quickly, and using his speed to angle away from pursuers reminded many observers of a young Marcus Allen. His 49 receptions for 367 yards also showed that he was an effective pass catcher. Missing the final two games probably cost him the NFL's Offensive Rookie of the Year Award, which went to his good friend, Curtis Martin. Davis finished second. *Football Digest*, however, selected Davis as its Offensive Rookie of the Year.

Despite the setbacks he had suffered in high school and college, Terrell Davis took nothing for granted and made the most of his opportunity with the Broncos. "My whole mentality is to expect the unexpected," he said. "There are no guarantees from one day to the next."[11]

Chapter 5

Race for the Rushing Title

In sports, if a player has a successful rookie year, sometimes that player will not be as successful in the second season. This phenomenon is known as the sophomore jinx. Davis, however, did not believe in this. "I don't believe in that junk," he said.

> People who go for that do well their first year then stop listening to people. They start believing their newspaper clips. They did well and don't work hard. I worked harder this off-season than ever.[1]

When the season started, it became obvious that Davis was not kidding about his work habits. In the first game of 1996 he ran for 72 yards and one touchdown as the Broncos crushed the visiting New York Jets, 31–6. That performance, however, turned out to be only a warm-up for the next four games. Against the Seattle Seahawks, Davis busted out for 111 yards on 28 carries to help Denver win, 30–20. Denver's 2–0 start had Davis excited about his team. "I believe this strongly in my heart: I don't think there's any team out there that can stop the Broncos," he said. "If we do the things we have to do—run the ball, throw the ball—we're the only ones that can stop us. And I seriously believe that."[2]

Even with a successful professional football career, Davis could not shake his migraines. In the second quarter of the third game of the season against the Tampa Bay Buccaneers, Davis became nauseated and blinded by a bright light. He knew it was a migraine and tried to stay in the game. But two plays later, Davis was forced to leave. "I didn't want anyone to know I had a migraine," he said, "but my vision started to get blurry. It got to the point where I couldn't see anything. It's more than a headache—you get weak, and the pain is unbelievable."[3]

Denver's trainers gave Davis some medicine, and fifteen minutes later the unbearable pain was gone. Denver was fortunate that Davis could return for the second half. He carried the ball eight times for 39 yards in a fourteen-play drive that consumed eight minutes and eleven seconds. Davis's 3-yard touchdown run up the middle with only three and a

FACT

During the New Year's Day holiday period, postseason bowl games take the place of an NCAA Division I-A tournament. Under the current format, the Big Ten Conference and Pacific Ten Conference champions meet in the Rose Bowl in Pasadena, CA, on New Year's Day. For the rest of Division 1-A, the fourth- and sixth-ranked teams play on New Year's Eve, the number three and five teams on January 1, and the number one and two teams on January 2. These three pairs of teams alternate playing in the Fiesta Bowl, the Orange Bowl, and the Sugar Bowl.

half minutes remaining gave the Broncos a 27–23 come-from-behind win. Davis finished the game with 137 yards on 22 carries.

The Kansas City Chiefs, the Western Division arch rival of the Denver Broncos, were next on Denver's schedule. Kansas City's head coach, Marty Schottenheimer, was impressed with Denver's second-year running back,

> Right now Davis may be the best back in the NFL, and that includes guys like Barry Sanders and Emmitt Smith. The guy is phenomenal. If he doesn't lose half a game [last week] to the migraine, he would probably lead the league in rushing. He's a powerful man with excellent vision. He has the strength of a fullback and the maneuverability of a halfback.[4]

Schottenheimer's words rang true as Davis ran 19 times for 141 yards and 2 touchdowns against the Chiefs. His 65-yard touchdown run in the second quarter gave Denver a 14–10 lead that lasted into the fourth quarter. Kansas City, however, managed to rally and win, 17–14. Despite his outstanding performance, Davis was disappointed. "We hurt ourselves," he said. "To beat a team like Kansas City or another powerhouse, you can't have mistakes."[5]

The Broncos bounced back against the Cincinnati Bengals. Davis ran for 112 yards on 24 carries, and John Elway threw for 335 yards and 2 touchdowns as Denver won, 14–10. Davis ran for 31 yards in the fourth quarter while the Broncos were protecting the lead. "There were just good enough holes for us to come through and get four or five yards a pop," he said. "That's what you want in the running game late in the game."[6]

It was the fourth consecutive game in which Davis broke the 100-yard barrier, tying a team record. For his outstanding play during the month of September, Davis won the AFC Offensive Player of the Month Award. He led the NFL with 573 rushing yards. Not surprisingly, Denver was off to a fast start at 4–1.

The entire Denver team appreciated the boost from a punishing ground attack. "In the past, we believed if we kept the game close, John [Elway] would do something to bail us out," said tight end Shannon Sharpe. "Now we can demoralize teams by running. . . ."[7] Fullback Aaron Craver agreed. "We're like the Redskins were with John Riggins," he said. "You knew they were going to run it, but could you stop them?"[8]

Another migraine slowed Davis against the San Diego Chargers. He had to leave the game in the second quarter, but he was able to return and rush for 45 of his 50 yards. Denver won, 28–17. A bad

In only his second year in the NFL, Terrell Davis was already being compared to the best running backs in the league, including the Cowboys' Emmitt Smith (shown here with the ball).

headache seemed the only thing capable of stopping Davis. This concerned Coach Shanahan. "His migraines make it very difficult for him to play, and I hope we can get them corrected," he said. "On the sideline during the second quarter I could see that he was not himself. He was in bad shape, came back in the second half, and frankly I could tell that he was playing with a lot of pain."[9]

Davis shook off the effects of the migraine and exploded for 194 yards on 28 attempts against the Baltimore Ravens. He also scored 2 touchdowns, including a 71-yarder in the first quarter. Denver won in a shoot-out, 45–34. Davis's 194 yards set a single-game Denver record, and his 71-yard touchdown run was the fourth longest in club history. Davis's phenomenal game earned him the AFC Offensive Player of the Week Award.

The following week in Denver's rematch with the Kansas City Chiefs, Davis became the quickest Broncos player to reach the 2,000 career-yard plateau. Denver avenged its loss from earlier in the season with a victory to improve its record to 7–1. The last time that the Broncos started a season 7–1 was 1986, a year they went to the Super Bowl. Davis was in the rare position of having an opportunity to lead the NFL in rushing *and* play in the Super Bowl.

Denver won its next two games to set up a

FACT

The American Professional Football Association (APFA) was organized in 1920. After one year it was reorganized. In 1922 it was renamed the National Football League (NFL). The NFL consists of two conferences, the American and the National, and at the end of each season the winners of the confer-ences play each other in the Super Bowl to determine the champion.

showdown against the New England Patriots in what many observers considered to be a preview of the AFC championship game. Davis came into the game with 1,055 yards. He was just the fourteenth player in NFL history to rush for 1,000 yards in each of his first two seasons. Reaching the 1,000-yard mark in the tenth game of the season was also a Denver record.

Against the Patriots, Davis started out strong and never looked back. Denver scored on its first three drives. Davis completed those drives with touchdown runs 10 and 2 yards along with a 15-yard touchdown reception. He finished the day with 32 carries for 154 yards and 3 touchdowns. Everything went Davis's way. En route to the end zone during his two-yard touchdown, he fumbled the ball but it bounced back into his hands. For the second time in 1996, Davis won the AFC Offensive Player of the Week Award.

"I guess today was my day," the humble Davis said after the 34–8 win. "I was getting a great push from my line. I had great lanes to run in and I just put my head down and got some extra yardage."[10]

Wins over the Minnesota Vikings and the Seattle Seahawks improved Denver's record to 12–1. The Broncos had won nine straight games and had the best record in the NFL. The victory over Seattle clinched the AFC Western Division title. In that game, Davis crossed the 100-yard mark for the seventh time of the season, tying a franchise record. "We knew we had a pretty good team going into the season," said Davis, whose 1,383 yards led the NFL with three games remaining. "We also knew we could be great, if we didn't beat ourselves. We can beat anybody out there. That's the mentality we have."[11]

After a loss to the Green Bay Packers, Denver bounced back with a 24–19 win over the Oakland Raiders. Davis contributed to the win with 80 yards rushing and a touchdown. The victory guaranteed Denver a first-round bye (week off) and home field advantage in the playoffs. The Broncos would play all of their postseason games at home.

With their playoff situation set, Davis could turn his attention to his personal goal of winning the NFL rushing title. Going into the final game of the season against the San Diego Chargers, Davis held a 96-yard lead over Pittsburgh's Jerome Bettis and a 139-yard lead over Detroit's Barry Sanders. Since 1990, either Sanders or Emmitt Smith had won the rushing crown. "It gives me a chance to break up the monotony," said Davis.[12] "I want it, without a doubt. This opportunity may never present itself again."[13]

Even with a fairly large lead, Davis knew it

would be difficult to win the rushing race. "I've pretty much had the lead all year, but you never know about [Bettis]," he said. "And Barry [Sanders] can come out and have a 250-yard game."[14]

Davis's words were prophetic. With a chance to make it to the Super Bowl, Coach Mike Shanahan did not want to risk injury to his star running back in a meaningless game. Davis carried the ball just nine times for 21 yards, giving him a season total of 1,538. Monday night, in the NFL's regular-season finale, however, Barry Sanders erupted for 175 yards against the San Francisco 49ers, giving him 1,553 yards and his third NFL rushing title. Davis had to settle for the AFC rushing crown. Now he could concentrate on the playoffs.

Denver's first playoff game was against the Jacksonville Jaguars. Jacksonville was an expansion team in its second year, and most experts expected the Broncos to win easily. Denver was favored by two touchdowns. With a 12-point first-quarter lead, it looked like the Broncos would put the game away early. Davis helped establish the lead with a 47-yard run to Jacksonville's 2-yard line. The run was a Denver playoff record. A few plays later, however, Davis suffered a knee sprain. After the injury, he gained only 42 more yards for a game total of 91 on just 14 carries.

In 1996, Terrell Davis lost the NFL rushing title to Detroit's Barry Sanders by only fifteen yards.

With Davis's effectiveness limited, the Jaguars mounted a spirited comeback and stunned the Broncos with a 30–27 upset. In an instant, Denver's season of promise was over. Davis and the Broncos were stunned. There would be no more playoff games—no Super Bowl. "I'm sick to my stomach," said Davis.[15]

The bitter playoff loss could not take away from Davis's outstanding season. He set numerous single-season records for the Broncos, including rushing yards (1,538), rushing attempts (345), total yards (1,848), and touchdowns (15). Davis was voted the NFL's Offensive Player of the Year by the Associated Press and the NFL Player of the Year by *Sports Illustrated*. His fellow players voted him a starter for the AFC Pro Bowl team. In just two years, Davis had gone from an unheralded draft pick to an NFL superstar.

Chapter 6

Running for the Super Bowl

Denver's nightmare ending to the 1996 season faded with the optimism of training camp, which opened six months after the playoff loss to Jacksonville. Terrell Davis literally dreamed of playing in Super Bowl XXXII. "I can actually visualize our team in terms of being at the Super Bowl," he said before the 1997 season. "I'm playing it in my head right now, and I'm trying to put every little factor together, and I'm saying, 'This has to be the year.'"[1]

Before Davis and the Broncos could seriously think about playing in the Super Bowl, they first had to play well during the regular season and qualify for the playoffs. Denver hoped to repeat as the AFC's Western Division champions and secure the home-field advantage throughout the playoffs. Those things, however, were easier said than done.

Denver's opening game was against the Kansas City Chiefs—the team's fiercest division rival. Strengthened by an aggressive defense and a strong running game, Denver came out on top 19-3. Davis ran the ball 26 times for 101 yards and one touchdown. He did not want to hear talk, however, about being in first place after only one game. "Come on now," said Davis. "This is a long season. We have a lot of games left. But it was encouraging to come away with a win today. We started off on the right foot."[2]

Davis continued his rushing pace with 107 yards against the Seattle Seahawks and 103 yards against the St. Louis Rams to help the Broncos to a 3–0 start. No one was more appreciative of a strong running game than John Elway. "It's like whenever we need to run the ball now, we can," the Denver quarterback said. "It's the Terrell Davis Show. I'm just happy to be in his world."[3]

Not content with his ho-hum 100-yard performances, Davis achieved a rare 200-yard game against the Cincinnati Bengals. He also made a key run in the 38–20 victory. On third and three at the 50-yard line with Denver leading 21–20, Davis shot through a huge hole on the left side of the offensive line. Cincinnati's free safety missed on his attempted tackle, and Davis went all the way for the score. "I felt if I could run in there hard and break a tackle or two, I would be out of the gate," he said. "I went in there with that mentality and, hey, came out with a 50-yard touchdown."[4]

Davis finished the game with 215 yards on the ground, a club record. He also topped the 3,000 career-yard mark in only his thirty-forth game, shattering the previous franchise record of 54 games. Not surprisingly, Davis won the AFC Offensive Player of the Week Award. The Broncos were now 4–0 for the third time in team history. Every other time the Broncos had gone undefeated after the first four games, the team reached the Super Bowl.

For the first time during the season, Davis was held to under 100 yards by the Atlanta Falcons. His 13-yard scoring scamper in the second quarter, along with his two 2-point conversion runs, however, helped the Broncos ease past the Falcons, 29–21. With 605 yards rushing for the season, Davis was first in the league. Like the previous September, his explosive start to the season earned him AFC Offensive Player of the Month honors.

The whole country got a glimpse of Davis's outstanding abilities in a televised Monday night game against the New England Patriots, the only

In a game against the Cincinnati Bengals in 1997, Terrell Davis set a franchise record with 215 rushing yards.

other unbeaten team in the NFL. Davis put on a show worthy of a national audience, carrying the ball 32 times for 171 yards and 2 touchdowns as the Broncos walloped the Patriots, 34–13. With an average of 129 yards per game, Davis was on pace for 2,069 yards, which would be the second highest single-season total in NFL history. "The guy is totally unique," said ESPN analyst Mark Malone. "You ask me who he reminds me of, and I'm at a loss, really. He's definitely very elusive, but he doesn't run like Barry Sanders. He's a very rare combination."[5]

The win over the Patriots put the Broncos at 6–0, tying the best start in club history. Denver had also opened the 1977 and 1986 seasons with six straight victories. Much of Denver's current success could be attributed to Davis, and he liked being the go-to guy. "As the game goes on, I get stronger and stronger," the third-year running back said. "It's like I'm in a zone. I like to get the ball in the fourth quarter."[6]

As they had during the previous season, Terrell Davis and Barry Sanders were running neck and neck for the NFL rushing title. "You never know what's going to happen next with him," Davis said of Sanders.

> You think Barry's getting caught for a 5-yard loss and then he's going for 80 yards. He

creates. He's like Michael Jordan. A lot of backs will take what they're given and are not able to make more out of [a carry]. But I don't care what type of [tackling] angle you have on him. He'll do the impossible.[7]

FACT

As of January 2000, Barry Sanders had played 10 seasons and rushed for 15,269 yards (trailing all-time leader Walter Payton, who rushed for 16,726 yards, by 1,457 yards). Sanders became the third player in NFL history to rush for more than 2,000 yards in a season by gaining a league-leading 2,053 yards in 1997. He won four rushing titles as of the 1998 season.

The Denver express hit a speed bump in a 28–25 loss to the Oakland Raiders before making a stop in Buffalo for a game against the Bills. To get back on the winning track, the Broncos looked to their star running back. Davis ended up carrying the ball a franchise-record 42 times for 207 yards and a touchdown. He also caught 5 passes for 29 yards as the Broncos eked out a 23–20 overtime win. "I feel it, man," said Davis.

> Forty-two carries. That's two games. I wouldn't want to keep that up. At this time in my rookie season, I was done. But I've been through two seasons and now I know what to expect. Mentally and physically, I think I can hold up for the season.[8]

Although he was in just his third year, Davis now held Denver's record for career 100-yard games with 16. This topped Floyd Little's mark of 15 games, which he set from 1967 to 1975. The record did not surprise tight end Shannon Sharpe. "Terrell Davis comes in and gets 120 yards a week. He could show up in street clothes and still get 120," said Sharpe.[9]

Many observers considered Davis to be the best running back in the NFL, even better than Emmitt Smith and Barry Sanders, but the comparison embarrassed Davis. "Emmitt has set the standard," said Davis.

> Year in and year out, he consistently puts up the yards even when they know he's going to get it, and most important of all, he's won championships. That's my ideal. He is the standard bearer for me and for any back who wants to be great. He's not God, but he's the goal we all shoot for and, ultimately, the person we use when we measure our own accomplishments.[10]

Following his 207-yard performance, Davis turned in three more 100-yard games. The Broncos won two of these games. The one loss came in Denver's rematch against the Kansas City Chiefs on a 54-yard field goal as time expired. If Davis could reach 100 yards in his next game against the Oakland Raiders, he would set Denver's record for consecutive 100-yard games. "He's one of the most devastating power backs that we face year in and year out," said Raiders head coach Joe Bugel. "The guy makes one cut and if you're not prepared for it, he can leave cleat marks all over your body. He's a premier back and commands a lot of attention, because he is a legitimate tough guy. If you don't get a lot of people to the ball, he can embarrass you."[11]

The Raiders went into the game with the goal of stopping Davis and continued their streak as the only AFC West team never to allow him to reach 100 yards. Oakland limited Davis to 69 yards. However, he scored 3 touchdowns, equaling Denver's' record for rushing touchdowns in a game. The Broncos stampeded the Raiders, 31–3, and improved to 10–2. "What else is new? They play [me] so tight," Davis said of Oakland's defense. "They have a guy sitting there and sort of stalking me. I have to be a little stronger this time of the year because you have a target on your back when you're the NFL's leading rusher. All they want to do is shut you down."[12]

Denver's next game was at San Diego. Thus far in his career, Davis had not had a breakout game in his hometown. That changed when he rushed for 178 yards on 26 carries. It was Davis's tenth 100-yard game of the season, a franchise record. Denver won, 38–28, to improve to 11–2.

The Broncos were the first AFC team to clinch a playoff spot. Their next two games, however, were also on the road as part of a rare three-game road trip. Winning at least one of the games was critical to ensure home-field advantage throughout the playoffs. That, however, would not be an easy task against the Pittsburgh Steelers and the San Francisco 49ers—two of the NFL's top teams.

Against the Steelers, the Broncos jumped out to a 21–7 lead. But Pittsburgh held Davis to 75 yards and came roaring back to win, 35–24. Denver was now tied with Kansas City for the AFC West lead. Unfortunately, things went from bad to worse in a Monday night matchup with the 49ers. Davis suffered a bruised shoulder in the second quarter after gaining just 28 yards on 10 carries, and Denver lost big, 34–17. To make matters worse, the Kansas City Chiefs won, giving them the AFC West crown and home-field advantage for the playoffs.

The shoulder injury suffered by Davis forced him to miss the final regular-season game against the San Diego Chargers. The Broncos, however, won to finish the season at 12–4. Denver qualified for the playoffs as a wild card. Since the wild card system was implemented in 1970, only four wild card teams had reached the Super Bowl. Only one of those teams, the 1980 Oakland Raiders, went on to win the Super Bowl.

Despite missing the last game, Davis had turned in one of the finest regular-season performances in Denver history. He led the AFC in rushing with 1,750 yards. (Barry Sanders led the NFL with 2,053, becoming just the third player to crack the 2,000-yard

In 1997, Terrell Davis set single-season franchise records in rushing yards, attempts, rushing touchdowns, total yards from scrimmage, and 100-yard games.

mark.) In addition to setting Denver's single-season record for rushing yards, Davis set team marks for attempts (369), rushing touchdowns (15), total yards from scrimmage (2,037), and 100-yard games (10). He rushed for more than 200 yards twice. Davis was just the eighth running back in NFL history to rush for 1,000 yards in each of his first three seasons.

Davis did not have time to think about his amazing season because the Broncos were in the playoffs. Denver's first game was at home against the Jacksonville Jaguars, the team that had knocked them out of the playoffs during the previous season. Davis continued his scorching rushing pace in the postseason. With Denver leading 21–17 in the third quarter, Davis exploded through the line of scrimmage for a 59-yard run. It was the longest run in Denver postseason history. Davis injured his ribs on the play and did not return to the game, but he still finished with 31 carries for 184 yards (both Denver playoff records) and 2 touchdowns. The Broncos went on to win, 42–17.

"There were some nice holes out there today," said Davis. "We just wanted to put the ball in the end zone."[13]

Kansas City was the next stop on Denver's march to the Super Bowl. The Broncos trailed in the fourth quarter, but Davis's second one-yard

FACT

A wild card is a team that does not win its division but still qualifies for the playoffs. In the current NFL system, three division winners and three wild cards from each conference make the playoffs.

touchdown run of the game put the team ahead, 14–10, for the win. He rushed for 70 of his 101 yards in the second half. The victory put Denver in the AFC championship game against the Steelers in Pittsburgh. A win there meant a trip to the Super Bowl.

The Steelers were a strong defensive team and had not allowed a player to rush for 100 yards all season. The Broncos, however, were determined to run the ball with Davis. He got off to a fast start. Just minutes into the game Davis broke free for a 43-yard gain. He capped the 72-play drive with an 8-yard touchdown run. He finished the game with 26 carries for 139 yards as Denver won, 24–21. Denver became the first wild card team to reach the Super Bowl since the 1992 Buffalo Bills. Denver defeated the Green Bay Packers in Super Bowl XXXII, 31–24, thanks in large part to Davis, who rushed for 157 yards. Denver was just the second wild card team to win the Super Bowl.

As night fell upon the Super Bowl, Davis grew stronger. He ran over Green Bay's defense in the final minutes of the game. Davis had spent the off-season working out daily to increase his strength and endurance. With his added strength, defensive backs had as much chance against him as a fly taking on a car windshield.

"The guy is an equalizer," said John Elway. "He means we're no longer one-dimensional and control the tempo of a game by wearing people down. When he's on, you can see the confidence of the defense eroding."[14]

Davis's postseason heroics equaled his regular-season feats. His 8 touchdowns were the most ever in NFL playoff history. He joined John Riggins as the only players to rush for 100 or more yards in four games in one postseason. Perhaps most impressive, Davis set the all-time NFL record for most rushing attempts (495) and rushing yards (2,331) in a regular season and postseason combined.

Chapter 7

The 2,000-Yard Man

Terrell Davis staged a storybook comeback in 1997. After being named the Super Bowl's Most Valuable Player (MVP), he became a national celebrity. Requests for interviews, television appearances, and endorsements were constant. He went to Disneyland, appeared on late-night television with Jay Leno and David Letterman, and met President Clinton at the White House.

Davis received an additional dose of notoriety immediately before training camp when he signed the most lucrative contract in Denver Broncos history, a nine-year deal that virtually guaranteed that he would be playing with the Broncos for the remainder of his career. At age twenty-five, Davis was the most eligible bachelor in the Rocky Mountain region.

"I don't want to play for eight million teams," Davis said regarding his new contract. "I want to be on one team. One day I want to have my jersey retired here. When people come to Denver, I want them to think of me."[1]

After three seasons in the NFL, Davis had rushed for 4,405 yards. The only players to rush for more during their first three years were Hall-of-Famers Eric Dickerson (5,147) and Earl Campbell (5,081). Like all professional athletes, however, Davis could not rest on his achievements. As he entered his fourth year in the NFL, football experts wondered whether he could continue to take the pounding he had endured in 1996 and 1997, when he racked up a monstrous total of 840 rushing attempts. Most running backs last a only few seasons in the NFL because of the wear and tear on their bodies, but Davis insisted that he felt fresh. "I don't want to hold back anything," Davis said. "I want to play as hard as I can for as long as I can. Once it's gone, it's gone. If I can play eight, nine years, I'll have no regrets."[2]

Davis faced the added pressure of being the best player on the defending Super Bowl champion team. Denver's opponents would be focusing on

Davis in every game. A team faces no greater challenge than defending its title. Other teams feel they can make a statement to the rest of the league by beating the champions. If the Denver Broncos thought it was difficult to win a Super Bowl, they were about to find out how tough it is to repeat such a feat.

Denver's first misstep of the season came under the white-hot spotlight of national television, a Monday night matchup against the New England Patriots. Having been burned by Davis's 422 yards in three previous games, the Patriots decided to concentrate on stopping the run. Davis wound up rushing for only 75 yards on 22 carries, but he scored 2 rushing touchdowns, a nine-yarder in the second quarter and a game-winning one-yarder in the fourth. The Broncos won, 27–21.

The Broncos next game pitted them against the Dallas Cowboys and their star running back, Emmitt Smith. Smith was someone Davis admired. "He's definitely been a back that I've looked up to for a long time," Davis said. "He reminds me of me a little bit because Emmitt's a short back, but he's still kind of powerful. He's not fast, like myself, but when he breaks a long run, he's capable of taking it all the way."[3]

Emmitt Smith returned the compliment. "In a lot

After he was named the Super Bowl MVP, Terrrell Davis became a national celebrity. He appeared with Jay Leno and David Letterman on late-night television and met President Bill Clinton at the White House.

of ways, he's like me. He's a north-and-south runner. In a lot of ways, I do see a young Emmitt Smith in him. I guess that's why I like him so much."[4]

Davis and Smith may be similar runners, but the Broncos and the Cowboys were about as similar as a lion and a kitten. Playing with computer-like precision, Denver came out and scored 5 touchdowns on its first five possessions. Davis provided two of the scores on runs of 63 and 59 yards. After one quarter, he had 138 yards on the ground. Davis finished the game with 191 yards and 3 touchdowns in the 42–23 win. Perhaps more impressive than how many yards he ran for was how easy he made it look.

On the first touchdown, Davis took the handoff from John Elway, cut left, beat linebacker Dexter Coakley, and outran the remaining Cowboys to the end zone. On the 59-yarder, Davis took a pitch left from Elway, cut back through the middle, and was gone.

"Just to be on the same field with him was incredible," said Cowboys All-Pro cornerback Deion Sanders. "He is a wonderful player."[5]

The game turned out to be the first of seven consecutive games in which Davis rushed for more than 100 yards. Even with Elway slightly injured, Denver won each of these games. The streak

FACT

Only four teams in pro football history have gone undefeated in a single season: the 1934 and 1942 Chicago Bears, the 1948 Cleveland Browns of the All-American Football Conference, and the 1972 Miami Dolphins. Only the Browns and Dolphins won championships.

included Davis's first-ever 100-yard day against the Oakland Raiders and a 208-yard performance, including a 70-yard run, against the Seattle Seahawks. He might have run for even more yards had he not sat out several quarters because the Broncos enjoyed big leads. Against the Philadelphia Eagles, he sat out the entire second half after rushing for 168 yards and scoring 2 touchdowns in the first half. For the month of September, Davis, who rushed for an NFL-leading 489 yards and 6 touchdowns, was selected the AFC Offensive Player of the Month.

With Denver sitting pretty at 8–0—the franchise's best start in its thirty-nine-year history—talk began about not only repeating as Super Bowl champions but also about the Broncos going undefeated. Davis and his teammates, however, did not want to admit that they were thinking about it. "There's only been one undefeated team in NFL history," said Davis. "We're not thinking about going undefeated right now. And it really doesn't matter if you go undefeated. If you go to the playoffs and lose, who cares?"[6]

With each rushing yard, Davis seemed to break another Denver record. In a 21–16 victory over the Seahawks, the fourth-year running back ran for his forty-fourth career rushing touchdown. That gave

At one point during the 1998 season, Terrell Davis rushed for more than 100 yards in seven consecutive games.

him one more than Floyd Little who had played for the Broncos from 1967 until 1975. In a 37–24 win over the Jacksonville Jaguars, Davis became just the third player in NFL history to rush for 1,000 yards in the first seven games of a season. Jim Brown (1958) and O. J. Simpson (1973 and 1975) are the other two.

Standard words of praise failed to capture Davis's abilities, so Shannon Sharpe came up with his own. "Terrell Davis is off to a Terrellian start," the outspoken tight end said of his favorite running back.[7]

With 1,150 yards after eight games, Davis was on pace to break the biggest prize of all for running backs, the NFL's single-season rushing record (2,105) set by former Ram Eric Dickerson in 1984. Besides Dickerson, only two other players had rushed for more than 2,000 yards: O. J. Simpson (2,003) in 1973 and Barry Sanders (2,053) in 1997. In a year in which Mark McGwire had broken baseball's most treasured record with 70 home runs, Davis's run for 2,000 yards seemed appropriate.

The month of October brought Davis two more awards. He was named the AFC Offensive Player of the Week for his 136-yard, 3-touchdown performance against the Jaguars. With 512 rushing yards for the month, Davis also won AFC Offensive Player of the Month honors.

Other running backs around the league began to consider Davis among the best. "A lot of backs try to out-do me," Davis said. "It's friendly competition. They want to look in the box score and say 'I out-rushed Terrell Davis.' I did that once with Emmitt Smith."[8]

After failing to gain 100 yards during Denver's 27–10 win over the San Diego Chargers, Davis bounced back with 111 yards, including a 41-yard touchdown run in a 30–7 rout of the Kansas City Chiefs. Davis now owned Denver's season records for touchdowns (17) and rushing touchdowns (16).

Marty Schottenheimer, head coach of the Kansas City Chiefs and an admirer of Davis since his rookie season, considered him one of the greatest running backs ever to play in the NFL. "He's got the toughness of a fullback and an innate running comparable to the great running backs in the history of the game," Schottenheimer said.[9]

The Broncos had a perfect 10–0 record. Davis had rushed for 1,330 yards, the most ever after ten games. He admitted that a 2,000-yard season was on his mind. "Human nature being what it is, sure you're going to think about it," said Davis. "When I'm out there playing, I don't think about 2,000 yards. When I come home and people mention it, then I do."[10]

A 40–14 win over the Oakland Raiders made the Denver Broncos the first defending Super Bowl champions to be 11–0. Davis helped the cause with 31 carries for 162 yards and one touchdown. In Denver's next game, a 31–16 victory over the San Diego Chargers that clinched the AFC Western Division title, Davis joined Barry Sanders as the only players in NFL history to rush for 1,500 yards in three consecutive seasons. Davis ran for 74 yards against the Chargers, but he did not consider it a bad game. "I look at my games to see if I did my assignments, whether I ran the ball hard, whether I caught passes and blocked," he explained. "I played a pretty good game and the statistics would indicate that."[11]

Denver pushed its record to 13–0 and earned home-field advantage throughout the playoffs with a 35–31 victory over the Kansas City Chiefs at Mile High Stadium. It was one of the most dramatic regular-season games in Broncos history. With eight minutes and twenty-five seconds remaining in the game, Denver trailed, 31–21. A 50-yard pass from Elway to wide receiver Willie Green put the ball on Kansas City's one-yard line. Davis's third rushing touchdown of the game cut Kansas City's lead to 31–28. A touchdown pass from John Elway to Shannon Sharpe on Denver's final possession gave

FACT

Dan Reeves is the NFL's winningest active coach with a career record of 177–136–1 in eighteen years, ranking ninth on the league's all-time list. His first head coaching job was with the Denver Broncos from 1981 until 1992. He led the Broncos to three Super Bowl appearances, but was defeated each time. After coaching the Broncos, Dan Reeves coached the New York Giants from 1993 until 1996. In 1997 took over as head coach of the Atlanta Falcons and, in 1998 became just the third head coach to lead two different teams to the Super Bowl. He has earned NFL Coach of the Year honors five times.

the team its eighteenth consecutive win, tying the 1933–1934 Bears, the 1941–1942 Bears, the 1972–1973 Dolphins, and the 1989–1990 49ers for the longest winning streak in NFL history.

A case of stomach flu could not stop Davis from rushing for 147 yards, including a 27-yard touchdown romp, against the New York Giants. Denver's dance with history, however, ended when the clock struck midnight on their undefeated season. Trailing 16–13 with forty-eight seconds remaining in the game, Giants wide receiver Amani Toomer caught a touchdown pass to give the Giants the win.

The loss not only cost the Broncos a place in history but also endangered Davis's chances of breaking Dickerson's single-season rushing record. He now needed to average 157 yards in the final two games to tie the record. Without the prospect of a perfect season, Coach Shanahan probably would not keep Davis in the game if the score was not close. "Regardless of what our record is," Davis said, "if we're up 20 points in those last two games, I don't think Mike would keep me in the game just to break a record."[12]

Davis's shot at 2,000 yards took a major blow during Denver's second consecutive defeat of the season when he rushed for a season-low 29 yards in a 28–3 loss to the Miami Dolphins. He now needed

170 yards in Denver's final regular-season game against the Seahawks to reach the 2,000-yard mark. Only one player—Jerome Bettis of the Pittsburgh Steelers—had rushed for 100 yards against Seattle that season.

With a chance to make history, Davis came out of the starting gate galloping. He ran for 10 yards on each of his first two carries. He ran for 54 yards in the first quarter, 28 in the second, and 51 in the third. When the Broncos took possession with ten minutes and thirty-nine seconds remaining in the game, Davis needed 31 yards. Mile High Stadium shook with the chant of Davis's initials, "T.D.! T.D.! T.D.! T.D.!"

Seattle's defense knew that Davis would be getting the ball. On first down, Davis ran off left tackle for 10 yards. He got 10 more off right guard. Then Davis ran up the middle for four more. On the next play, he took the handoff and ran around left end for 15 yards into the record book. Davis became the fourth running back in NFL history to run for 2,000 yards in one season. He finished the day with 178 yards and 2,008 for the season, the third-highest total in NFL history. Denver's 28–21 win became a footnote.

"I was hoping on the first play to get a lot of yards," a smiling Davis said after the game. "I got

In 1998, Terrell Davis became only the fourth player in NFL history to rush for 2,000 yards in a season.

10, and I got really excited. The next play I got 10 more and got even more excited. It was pretty wild in the huddle. You should've been there."[13]

After setting a franchise-record with 14 regular-season wins, the Broncos turned their attention to winning their second consecutive Super Bowl. Their first playoff opponent was the Miami Dolphins, who had already defeated Denver during the regular season. Behind Davis, who carried the ball 21 times for 199 yards and 2 touchdowns, the Broncos demolished the Dolphins 38–3 and advanced to the AFC championship game against the New York Jets.

A one-yard touchdown run by Curtis Martin, Davis's good friend, gave the Jets a 10–0 lead in the third quarter. The Broncos, however, scored 20 points in the third quarter, including a 31-yard touchdown run by Davis. He finished the game with 167 yards on 32 carries. A fourth-quarter field goal by Denver kicker Jason Elam rounded out the scoring, and the Broncos were on their way to a second straight Super Bowl.

In the Super Bowl the year before, the Broncos had been underdogs. In Super Bowl XXXIII, they were favored to beat the Atlanta Falcons, who were making their first Super Bowl appearance. With 102 yards on 25 carries and 50 yards on 2 catches, Davis helped Denver build a 31–6 lead by the fourth quarter. The final score was 34–16, giving the Broncos their second Super Bowl title. Atlanta focused on stopping Davis, which allowed John Elway to throw for 336 yards and one touchdown to earn his first Super Bowl MVP award.

"I knew it was going to be tough," Davis said after his NFL-record seventh consecutive post-season 100-yard rushing game. "We have a lot of people on this team. When you stop our running game, you have to deal with our passing game. John was really on today."[14]

Davis's fairy-tale season had helped the Broncos win another championship. In addition, Davis had finally won the NFL rushing title, and in the process, became Denver's all-time leading rusher (6,413 yards). He set franchise season records for rushing yards, total yards (2,225), carries (392), rushing touchdowns (21), and total touchdowns (23). Davis won the Associated Press's Most Valuable Player and Offensive Player of the Year honors.

Chapter 8

Mama's Boy

Terrell Davis is one of the best running backs in the NFL. Off the field, however, he carries himself more like an offensive lineman—quiet, unassuming, and humble. After a game, Davis is likely to be at home getting ready for bed. Take the night of Denver's Super Bowl XXXII victory in January 1998. Team owner Pat Bowlen threw a big party. The Super Bowl MVP, however, was nowhere in sight. He was asleep in his hotel room. "I try to keep my life as simple as possible," he said. "I try not to complicate it with all this football-star stuff."[1] Davis's mom added, "He has not changed. He's not arrogant. He's not like, 'I'm better than somebody else.' That's good."[2]

When endorsement deals poured in following

FACT

First aired on November 10, 1969, *Sesame Street* was designed to use television to teach preschoolers basic skills. It combined education along with entertainment. *Sesame Street* has received the most Emmys in television history. As for the show's title, the name "Sesame" was meant to conjure up a sense of excitement and adventure, as in the Arabian Nights command, "Open Sesame!"

Super Bowl XXXII, Davis immediately accepted the one he believed in most strongly, although it was not as lucrative as other offers. He became a spokesman for Novartis Pharmaceuticals, which produces a drug to relieve the effects of migraine headaches. During the 1998 off-season, Davis presided over headache seminars in ten cities.

Davis did not stop his community involvement there. After signing a new contract with the Denver Broncos before the 1998 season, he formed the Terrell Davis Salutes the Kids Foundation. Davis's mom is the foundation's president. The foundation, according to her, is "devoted to helping children, and providing assistance to families with children by contributing to their psychological, physical and social well-being through grants, scholarships and programs that recognize, reward, or facilitate their efforts and achievements."[3]

"In this world," Davis added, "everything evolves and starts with children. I love kids. They're the ones who are going to be our future leaders. They can be molded and shaped. Right now, we can really affect them."[4]

Davis takes his position as a role model for kids seriously. Near the end of the 1998 season, he agreed to appear in a thirtieth anniversary showing of *Sesame Street*, was interviewed for a feature article in

Terrell Davis tries to be a good role model. He formed the Terrell Davis Salutes the Kids Foundation, which is devoted to helping children.

Scholastic magazine, and wrote an advice column in *Sports Illustrated for Kids*. Davis' primary advice to kids is to work hard and persevere. "When a person goes through a lot of setbacks in life, it builds you as a person," Davis said.[5]

When not playing football, Davis spends a lot of time with his family. He bought his mother a home near him in suburban Denver. Davis is a famous football player adored by millions, but he is still very close to his mom. Kateree Davis is very active in her son's career. She and other mothers of professional football players formed the Professional Football Players Association. She says their mission is,

> to support our sons and their families by developing programs to enhance their continued professional and social successes while emphasizing good character, athletic excellence, and positive images through community service.[6]

One of the keys to Davis's success is his ability to put football before fame and fortune. He realizes how fortunate he is and takes nothing for granted. "I've come from nowhere," Davis said. "That's a big motivation. I've never been pampered. I've never been on a team where everybody looked at me as one of their weapons."[7]

As the 2000 NFL season approaches, Terrell

Davis finds himself in the position of having to prove himself all over again. During the Broncos fourth game of the 1999 season, he suffered torn ligaments and cartilage in his right knee and missed the remainder of the season. Without Davis and John Elway, who retired after Denver's second Super Bowl victory, the Broncos went 6–10 and finished in last place in the AFC West.

Although knee injuries are not necessarily career ending, as they once were, Davis wonders how his knee will respond to rehabilitation. You're always curious what's going to happen next," he said "Can it take this or that or that? I think that's going to happen until I get hit in practice."[8]

Davis also will be fighting to regain his starting position. Olandis Gary, who like Davis played college football at Georgia, gained 1,100 yards in twelve games. "Every year, I approach it the same way—I could lose my job," Davis said. "Go out there and produce, the job is mine. If I don't produce, I don't deserve to be there."[9]

Chapter Notes

Chapter 1. Super Bowl MVP

1. "Speedy Relief and an Exhilarating Comeback from Migraines," *U.S. News & World Report*, February 9, 1998, <http://www.usnews. com> (July 1, 1999).

2. Bill Plaschke, "In the End, He Gave Packers a Headache," *The Los Angeles Times*, January 26, 1998, <http://www.latimes.com> (July 1, 1999).

3. Austin Murphy, "Unstoppable," *Sports Illustrated*, February 2, 1998, <http://cnnsi.com> (July 1, 1999).

4. Plaschke, <http://www.latimes.com>

5. "Davis' Reward: Super Bowl MVP," *The Sporting News*, January 26, 1998, <http://www. sportingnews.com> (July 1, 1999).

6. Larry Weisman, "Elway Hands the Football and the Praise to Davis," *USA Today*, January 26, 1998, p. 2C.

7. Jon Sarceno, "MVP Davis a Headache to Packers," *USA Today*, January 26, 1998, p. 1C.

Chapter 2. Boss Hogg

1. Len Pasquarelli, "Hidden Talents," *The Atlanta Journal and Constitution*, January 21, 1998, <http://www.ajc.com> (July 1, 1999).

2. Terrell Davis with Adam Schefter, *TD: Dreams in Motion* (New York: HarperCollins, 1998), p. 72.

3. Bob Kravitz, "If You're Scoring at Home, T.D.'s the Best," *Rocky Mountain News*, October 7, 1997, <http://www.rockymountainnews.com> (July 1, 1999).

4. Mark Wolf, "Davis Not Crying for Chargers Now," *Rocky Mountain News*, November 20, 1995, <http://www.rockymountainnews.com> (May 1, 1998).

5. Clay Latimer, "The Tough-Luck Kid Catches a Break," *Football Digest*, March 1996, p. 32.

6. Clay Latimer, "Longshot Davis Rides to Elway's Rescue," *Joe Theisman's Pro Football Yearbook '96*, 1996, p. 81.

7. Jack Etkin, "Lincoln High Shows Its Pride in T.D.," *Rocky Mountain News*, January 21, 1998, <http://www.rockymountainnews.com> (July 1, 1999)

8. Bob Kravitz, "T.D. Comes Home a Hero to the Mean Streets He Escaped," *Rocky Mountain News*, January 19, 1998, <http://www.rockymountainnews.com> (July 1, 1999).

9. Don Norcross, "Chargers Fan Now the Darling of Denver," *The San Diego Union-Tribune*, September 23, 1995, <http://www.uniontrib.com> (July 1, 1999).

10. Davis with Schefter, p. 82.

11. Kravitz, "T.D. Comes Home a Hero to the Mean Streets He Escaped."

Chapter 3. Georgia On His Mind

1. Austin Murphy, "Late Bloomer," *Sports Illustrated*, October 28, 1996, pp. 56–57.

2. Terrell Davis and Vickie Bane, "Coping," *People*, December 23, 1996, <http://www.pathfinder.com/people> (July 1, 1999).

3. William F. Reed, "Inside College Football," *Sports Illustrated*, November 1, 1993, <http://cnnsi.com> (July 1, 1999).

4. Clay Latimer, "Longshot Davis Rides to Elway's Rescue," *Joe Theisman's Pro Football Yearbook '96*, 1996, p. 81.

5. Tom Maloney, "Davis Looks to Impress Scouts," *The San Diego Union-Tribune*, December 25, 1994, <http://www.uniontrib.com> (July 1, 1999).

6. Joe Strauss, "Terrell Davis Down on Dog Days," *The Atlanta Journal and Constitution*, November 16, 1996, <http://www.ajc.com> (July 2, 1999).

7. Tom Maloney, "Davis Looks to Impress Scouts," *The San Diego Union-Tribune*, December 25, 1994, <http://www.uniontrib.com> (July 1, 1999).

8. Terrell Davis and Adam Schefter, *TD: Dreams in Motion* (New York: HarperCollins, 1998), p. 95.

9. Curtis Bunn, "Terrell Davis: Mile High High Stepper," *The Atlanta Journal and Constitution*, September 26, 1997, <http://www.ajc.com> (July 1, 1999).

10. Paul Newberry, "Small-Time Stars Show Big-Time Potential," *The San Diego Union-Tribune*, December 26, 1994, <http://www.uniontrib.com> (July 1, 1999).

11. David Scott, "Fast Friends," *Sports Illustrated For Kids*, December 1, 1997, <http://www.sikids. com> (July 1, 1999).

12. Ibid.

13. Clay Latimer. "The Tough-Luck Kid Catches a Break," *Football Digest*, March 1996, p. 32.

14. Austin Murphy, "Late Bloomer," *Sports Illustrated*, October 28, 1996, p. 57.

Chapter 4. Rookie

1. Steve Weiberg, "AFC Notes," *USA Today*, August 16, 1995, <http://www.usatoday.com> (July 1, 1999).

2. Pete Dougherty, "Broncos' Low Draft Pick a Winner," *Gannett News Service*, December 3, 1996, <http://www.electroniclibrary.com> (July 1, 1999).

3. Don Norcross, "Chargers Fan Now the Darling of Denver," *The San Diego Union-Tribune*, September 23, 1995, <http://www.uniontrib.com> (July 1, 1999).

4. Clay Latimer, "No Turning Back," *Rocky Mountain News*, September 28, 1997, <http://www.rockymountainnews.com> (July 1, 1999).

5. Don Norcross, "Seau Shakes Off Muff With Pair of Big Plays," *The San Diego Union-Tribune*, September 25, 1995, <http://www.uniontrib.com> (July 1, 1999).

6. John Walters, "NFL Plus," *Sports Illustrated*, October 30, 1995, <http://cnnsi.com> (July 1, 1999).

7. Dale Bublitz, "As a San Diego Native, Terrell Davis was a Chargers Fan," *Gannett News Service*, November 19, 1995, <http://www.electroniclibrary.com> (July 1, 1999).

8. "Denver Broncos Team Notes," *The Sports Network*, September 13, 1996, <http://www.electroniclibrary.com> (July 1, 1999).

9. John Walters, "NFL Plus," *Sports Illustrated*, November 27, 1995, <http://cnnsi.com> (July 1, 1999).

10. Don Norcross, "Elway? Terrell's Way," *The San Diego Union-Tribune*, November 20, 1995, <http://www.uniontrib.com> (July 1, 1999).

11. Don Norcross, "Chargers Fan Now the Darling of Denver," *The San Diego Union-Tribune*, September 23, 1995, <http://www.uniontrib.com> (July 1, 1999).

Chapter 5. Race for the Rushing Title

1. "Denver Broncos Team Notes," *The Sports Network*, September 13, 1996, <http://www.electroniclibrary.com> (July 1, 1999).

2. Kelly Carter, "Broncos Topple Seahawks 30-20," *USA Today*, September 9, 1996, <http://www.usatoday.com> (July 1, 1999).

3. "Elway, Broncos Rely on Davis," *The Los Angeles Times*, September 16, 1996, <http://www.latimes.com> (July 1, 1999).

4. "Kansas City Chiefs Notes," *The Sports Network*, September 20, 1995, <http://www.electroniclibrary.com> (July 1, 1999).

5. Jarrett Bell, "Rival Broncos Cannot Capitalize on Opportunities to Beat Chiefs," *USA Today*, September 23, 1996, <http://www.usatoday.com> (July 1, 1999).

6. "Broncos' Elway Takes to the Air," *The Los Angeles Times*, September 30, 1996, <http://www.latimes.com> (July 1, 1999).

7. Peter King, "Inside the NFL," *Sports Illustrated*, October 23, 1996, p. 74.

8. Ibid.

9. "Denver Broncos Team Notes," *The Sports Network*, October 8, 1996, <http://www.electroniclibrary.com> (July 1, 1999).

10. Bill Tavares, "Denver 34, New England 8," *Gannett News Service*, November 17, 1996, <http://www.electroniclibrary.com> (July 1, 1999).

11. Jarrett Bell, "Broncos Not About to Ease Up," *USA Today*, November 26, 1996, <http://www.usatoday.com> (July 1, 1999).

12. Jarrett Bell, "Gift-Giving on the Line for Broncos' Davis," *USA Today*, December 19, 1996, <http://www.usatoday.com> (July 1, 1999).

13. Clay Latimer, "Rush Title Beckons to Davis," *The San Diego Union-Tribune*, December 20, 1996, <http://www.uniontrib.com> (July 1, 1999).

14. Ibid.

15. Rick Reilly, "NFL Playoffs," *Sports Illustrated*, January, 13, 1997, <http://cnnsi.com> (July 1, 1999).

Chapter 6. Running for the Super Bowl

1. "The Bottom Line," *The Sporting News*, January 17, 1998, <http://www.sportingnews.com> (July 1, 1999).

2. Alex Marvez, "Best in West," *Rocky Mountain News*, September 1, 1997, <http://www. rockymountainnews.com> (July 1, 1999).

3. Curtis Eichelberger, "Running for a Little Glory," *Rocky Mountain News*, September 9, 1997, <http://www.rockymountainnews.com> (July 1, 1999).

4. Alex Marvez, "Looking Fine at 4-0," *Rocky Mountain News*, September 22, 1997, <http://www.rockymountainnews.com> (July 2, 1999).

5. Bob Kravitz, "If You're Scoring at Home, T.D.'s the Best," *Rocky Mountain News*, October 7, 1997, <http://www.rockymountainnews.com> (July 2, 1999).

6. "Denver Wins Battle of Unbeatens," National Football League Web site, October 6, 1997, <http://www.nfl.com>, (July 2, 1999).

7. Alex Marvez, "Davis Bows to Sanders," *Rocky Mountain News*, October 19, 1997, <http://www.rockymountainnews.com> (July 2, 1999).

8. Clay Latimer, "Davis Hones Body," *Rocky Mountain News*, October 28, 1997, <http://www.rockymountainnews.com> (July 2, 1999).

9. "Gordon Leads Denver Rout," National Football League Web site, November 9, 1997, <http://www.nfl.com/news/97recaps/week11/carden.html> (July 2, 1999).

10. Eichelberger, "Running for a Little Glory."

11. Alex Marvez, "Broncos Ready to Respond," *Rocky Mountain News*, November 24, 1997, <http://www.rockymountainnews.com> (July 2, 1999).

12. Clay Latimer, "Home Improvement," *Rocky Mountain News*, November 30, 1997, <http://www.rockymountainnews.com> (July 2, 1999).

13. "Jaguars Trampled in Broncos Stampede," National Football League Web site, December 27, 1997, <http://www.nfl.com/news/97recaps/week18/jacden.html> (July 2, 1999).

14. Len Pasquarelli, "Blue Collar vs. High Tech," *The Atlanta Journal and Constitution*, January 11, 1998, <http://www.ajc.com> (July 2, 1999).

Chapter 7. The 2,000-Yard-Man

1. Adam Schefter, "Davis NFL's Top-Paid Runner," *Denver Post*, July 24, 1998, <http://www.denverpost.com> (July 24, 1998).

2. Paul Domowitch, "Migraine Couldn't Slow Down Super Bowl MVP, Then or Now," *Philadelphia Daily News*, May 20, 1998, p. 70.

3. Joseph Sanchez, "Terrell Says No. 22 'Reminds Me of Me'," *Denver Post*, September 13, 1998, <http://www.denverpost.com> (September 13, 1998).

4. Joseph Sanchez, "Cowboys See 'A Young Emmitt Smith' in Davis," *Denver Post*, September 13, 1998, <http://www.denverpost.com> (September 13, 1998).

5. Lynn Zinser, "Broncos Crush 'Boys, Aikman," *Philadelphia Daily News*, September 14, 1998, p. 114.

6. Phil Gianficaro, "Undefeated Talk Creeping Up on Broncos," *Philadelphia Inquirer*, October 4, 1998, p. C12.

7. Tony Jackson, "Broncos Rush to Find Words for Davis, *Rocky Mountain News*, October 13, 1998, <http://www.rockymountainnews.com> (October 13, 1998).

8. Irv Moss, "Speed Bump in Davis' Record Rush," *Denver Post*, October 30, 1998, <http://www.denverpost.com> (October 30, 1998).

9. Patrick Saunders, "Davis Has Schott at Being Best Ever," *Denver Post*, November 12, 1998, <http://www.denverpost.com> (November 12, 1998).

10. Patrick Saunders, "Davis Still on a Record Groove," *Denver Post*, November 18, 1998, <http://www.denverpost.com> (November 18, 1998).

11. Joseph Sanchez, "Yards Grow Longer in Pursuit," *Denver Post*, December 3, 1998, <http://www.denverpost.com> (December 3, 1998).

12. Jim Armstrong, "Davis Effort Nauseated," *Denver Post*, December 14, 1998, <http://www.denverpost.com> (December 14, 1998).

13. Adam Schefter, "Needed 170, Ran for 178," *Denver Post*, December 28, 1998, <http://www.denverpost.com> (December 28, 1998).

14. Jeff Hamrick, "Davis Yields Center Stage," *Denver Post*, February 1, 1999, <http://www.denverpost.com> (February 1, 1999).

Chapter 8. Mama's Boy

1. Mark Kiszla, "No Quit in Davis' Hopes," *Denver Post*, May 3, 1998, <http://www.denverpost.com> (May 3, 1998).

2. Adam Schefter, "Terrell Still Calls On His Mom," *Denver Post*, January 27, 1999, <http://denverpost.com> (January 27, 1999).

3. Adam Schefter, "Paybacks Are Swell for T.D.'s Kids," *Denver Post*, July 24, 1998, <http://www.denverpost.com> (July 24, 1998).

4. Ibid.

5. Carol Kreck, "Terrell Davis Has a Message for Kids," *Denver Post*, January 18, 1999, <http://www.denverpost.com> (January 18, 1999).

6. Adam Schefter, "NFL Moms Lend Helping Handoff," *Denver Post*, July 18, 1998, <http://www.denverpost.com> (July 18, 1998).

7. Joe Strauss, "Terrell Davis Down on Dog Days," *The Atlanta Journal and Constitution*, November 16, 1996, <http://www.ajc.com> (July 2, 1999).

8. Luke Cyphers, "All the Way Back," *ESPN Magazine*, February 21, 2000, p. 70.

9. Ibid.

Career Statistics

Year	Team	G	GS	ATT	YRDS	AVG	TD	REC	YRDS	AVG	TD
1995	Broncos	14	14	237	1,117	4.7	7	49	367	7.5	1
1996	Broncos	16	16	345	1,538	4.5	13	36	310	8.6	2
1997	Broncos	15	15	369	1,750	4.7	15	42	287	6.8	0
1998	Broncos	16	16	392	2,008	5.1	21	25	217	8.7	2
1999	Broncos	4	4	67	211	3.1	2	3	26	8.7	0
Totals		65	65	1,410	6,624	4.7	58	155	1,207	7.8	5

G—Games   **GS**—Games Started   **ATT**—Attempts   **YRDS**—Yards
AVG—Average   **TD**—Touchdowns   **REC**—Receptions

Where to Write Terrell Davis

Terrell Davis
c/o Denver Broncos
13655 Broncos Parkway
Englewood, CO 80112

On the Internet at:

Official NFL Web site
<http://www.nfl.com>

Official Denver Broncos Web site
<http://www.denverbroncos.com>

Index

Long Beach State, 23–27, 29
Longwell, Ryan, 11
lupus, 18, 21

M

Malone, Mark, 63
Martin, Curtis, 32–34, 39, 46, 85
McGwire, Mark, 79
Miami Dolphins, 76, 82, 84
migraine, 7–9, 11, 20, 26, 49, 53, 88
Minnesota Vikings, 54
Mobley, John, 15
Morse High School, 21, 22

N

New England Patriots, 33, 34, 39, 54, 61, 63, 74
New York Giants, 26, 82
New York Jets, 34, 48, 84, 85

O

Oakland Raiders, 55, 64, 65–67, 77, 81

P

Payton, Walter, 19, 64
Pennington, Jemaul, 29
Philadelphia Eagles, 76
Pittsburgh Steelers, 67, 70, 83
Player, Vic, 16, 17, 21, 22

R

Riggins, John, 51, 71
Reeves, Dan, 82
Robinson, Eugene, 12
Ryan, Buddy, 41

S

Sacca, John, 32
San Diego Chargers, 18, 39, 42, 43, 51, 55, 66, 67, 79–81
San Francisco 49ers, 37, 56, 67, 82

Sanders, Barry, 50, 55–57, 63–65, 67, 79, 81
Sanders, Deion, 76
Seattle Seahawks, 45, 46, 49, 54, 60, 77, 83
Sesame Street, 88
Schottenheimer, Marty 50, 80
Shanahan, Mike, 8, 36, 37, 40, 43, 53, 82
Sharpe, Shannon, 8, 14, 51, 64, 79, 81
Simpson, O.J., 18, 79
Smith, Emmitt, 52, 55, 65, 74, 76, 80

T

Tampa Bay Buccaneers, 49
Terrell Davis Salutes the Kids Foundation, 88, 89
Terrell, Tammi, 17
Toomer, Amani, 82

U

University of Arizona, 25
University of Arkansas, 28
University of Pittsburgh, 32, 33
University of Tennessee, 28, 29

W

Walker, Herschel, 26, 30
Warren, Chris, 45
Washington Redskins, 24, 38
West Coast Offense, 26
White, Frank, 17
wild card, 67, 69
Williams, Brian, 14
Williams, Tyrone, 14

Z

Zeier, Eric, 31